LOVE SONGS

Music arranged and processed by Barnes Music Engraving Ltd, East Sussex TN22 4HA, England
Cover design by xheight Limited
Published 1996

IMP

I JUST CALLED TO SAY I LOVE YOU

Words and Music by STEVIE WONDER

Registration
Upper: (Verse) Harmonica, (Chorus) Pop Organ
Lower: Organ / Strings
Pedal: 8' Bass Guitar
Rhythm   8 Beat
Tempo   ♩ = 116

I CAN'T GIVE YOU ANYTHING BUT LOVE

Words by DOROTHY FIELDS
Music by JIMMY McHUGH

Registration
Upper: Pop Organ
Lower: Organ 8' 4'
Pedal: 8' Acoustic Bass
Rhythm Bright Swing (Jazz Swing)
Tempo ♩ = 160

7

I'LL BE THERE

Words and Music by BERRY GORDY, HAL DAVIES, WILLIE HUTCH and BOB WEST

Registration
Upper: Pop Organ or Guitar / Strings
Lower: Piano / Strings
Pedal: 8' Acoustic Bass
Rhythm 8 Beat
Tempo ♩ = 90

8

9

LOVE IS HERE TO STAY

Music and Lyrics by GEORGE GERSHWIN and IRA GERSHWIN

Registration
Upper: Vibes / Guitar / Piano
Lower: Piano / Strings
Pedal: 8' Acoustic Bass
Rhythm   Swing
Tempo   ♩ = 108

11

KILLING ME SOFTLY WITH HIS SONG

Words and Music by NORMAN GIMBEL and CHARLES FOX

Registration
Upper: (Verse) Electric Piano, (Chorus) Pan Flute
Lower: Organ / Strings
Pedal: 8' Acoustic Bass
Rhythm Bossa Nova
Tempo ♩ = 100

1. I heard he sang a good song,
   I heard he had a style.
   And so I came to see him to
   listen for a while.
   And there he was this young boy
   a stranger to my eyes.

2. I felt all flushed with fever,
   em-bar-assed by the crowd.
   I felt he found my letters and
   read each one out loud.
   I prayed that he would fin-ish
   but he just kept right on.

3. He sang as if he knew me,
   in all my dark des-pair.
   And then he looked right thru me as
   if I was-n't there.
   But he was there this stran-ger
   sing-ing clear and strong.

15

LET'S DO IT (Let's Fall In Love)

Words and Music by COLE PORTER

LOVE IS A MANY-SPLENDOURED THING

Words by PAUL FRANCIS WEBSTER
Music by SAMMY FAIN

Registration	
Upper:	Vibraphone / Strings
Lower:	Organ / Strings
Pedal:	8' Acoustic Bass
Rhythm	Shuffle or Swing
Tempo	♩ = 110

MY FOOLISH HEART

Words by NED WASHINGTON
Music by VICTOR YOUNG

Registration
Upper: Orch. Strings / Flute
Lower: Piano / Strings
Pedal: 8' Acoustic Bass
Rhythm   Beguine
Tempo   ♩ = 95

TENDERLY

Words by JACK LAWRENCE
Music by WALTER GROSS

Registration
Upper: Strings / Solo Violin
Lower: Strings / Piano
Pedal: 8' Acoustic Bass
Rhythm   Waltz
Tempo   ♩ = 86

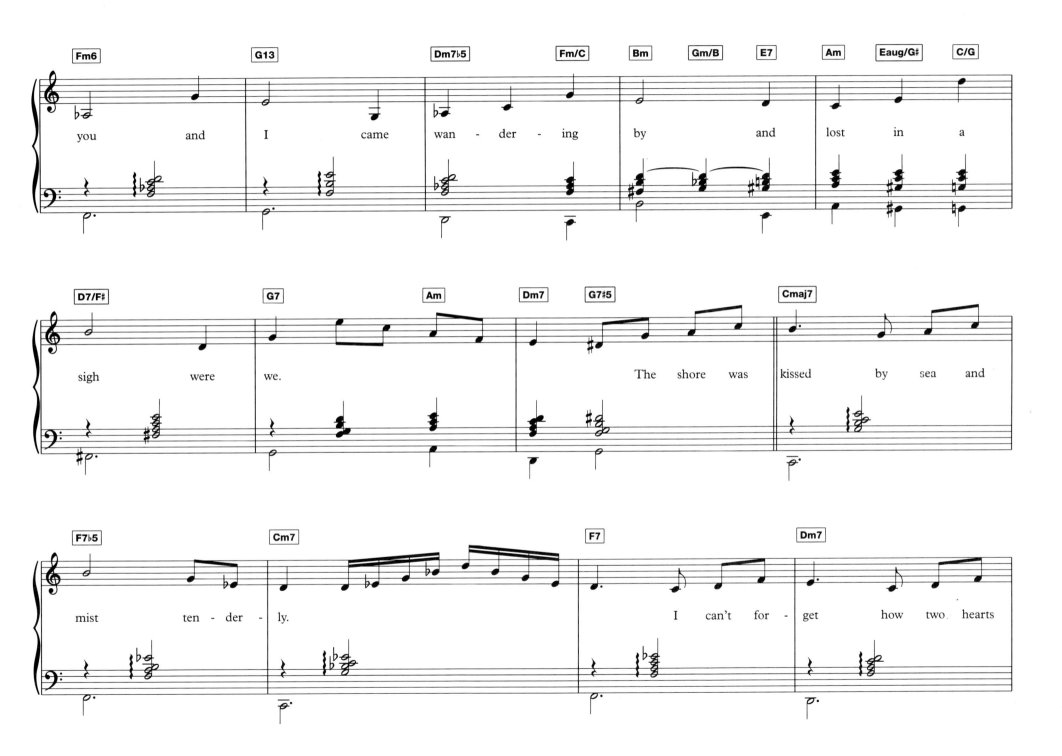

THREE TIMES A LADY

Words and Music by LIONEL RICHIE

Registration
Upper: Pop Organ
Lower: Piano / Strings
Pedal: 8' Electric Bass
Rhythm   Waltz or Jazz Waltz
Tempo   ♩ = 85

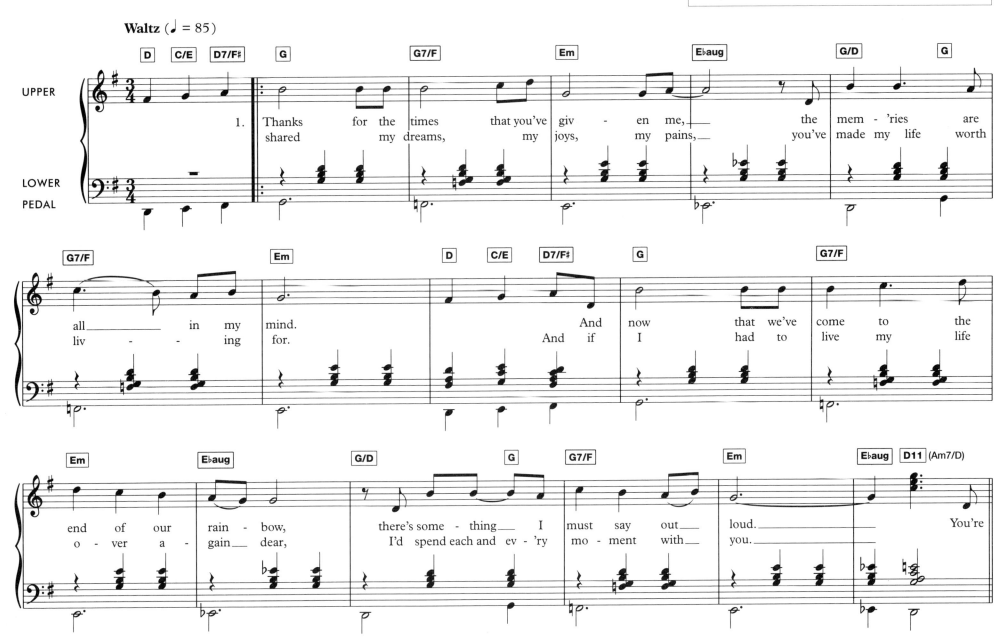

once, twice, three times a lady, and I love you.

Yes, you're once, twice, three times a lady,

and I love you, ooh, I love you,

Verse 3:
(When) we are together
The moments I cherish,
With ev'ry beat of my heart.
To touch you, to hold you,
To feel you, to need you,
There's nothing to keep us apart.

TOO MARVELLOUS FOR WORDS

Words by JOHNNY MERCER
Music by RICHARD A WHITING

Registration
Upper: Brass or Saxophone
Lower: Brass / Piano
Pedal: 8' Electric Bass
Rhythm Big Band Swing
Tempo ♩ = 155

UP WHERE WE BELONG

Words by WILL JENNINGS

Music by BUFFY SAINTE-MARIE and JACK NITZSCHE

Registration
Upper: Electric Piano / Guitar
Lower: Piano / Strings
Pedal: Funk Bass
Rhythm   16 Beat
Tempo   ♩ = 72

31

THE WAY YOU LOOK TONIGHT

Words by DOROTHY FIELDS
Music by JEROME KERN

Registration	
Upper:	(Chorus) Vibraphone, (Bridge) Trombone
Lower:	Electric Piano / Strings
Pedal:	8' Acoustic Bass
Rhythm	Bounce or Swing
Tempo	♩ = 100

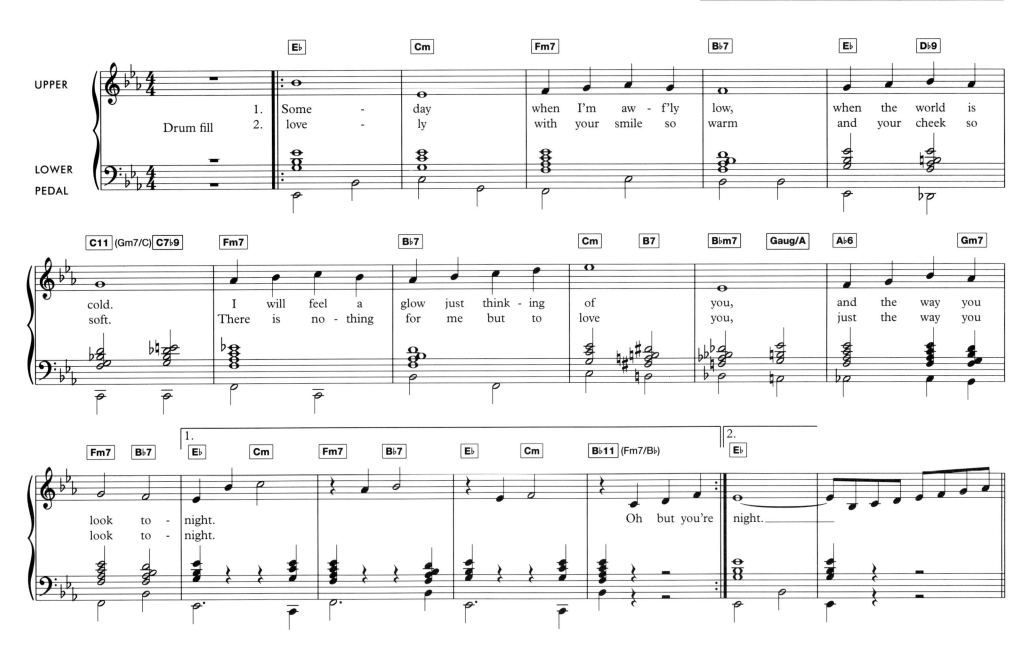

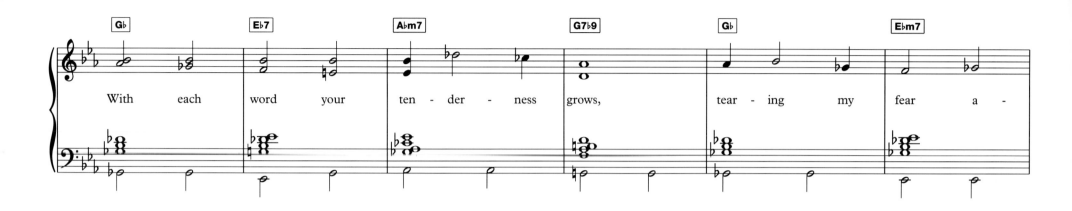

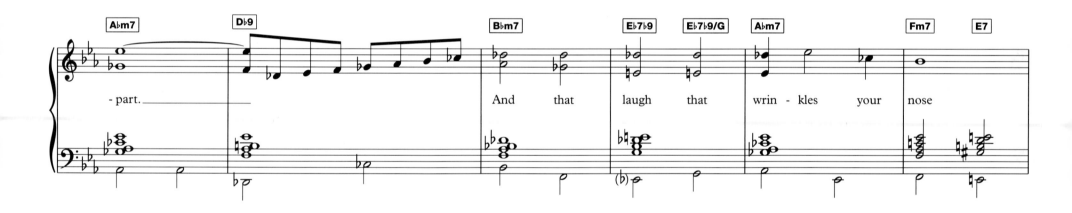

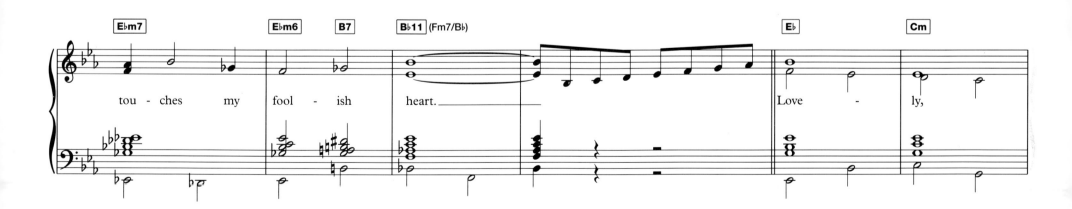

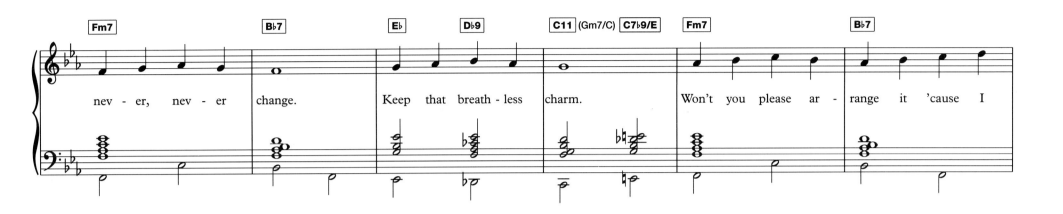

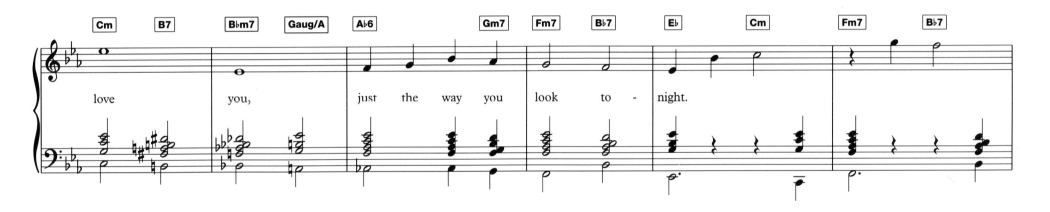

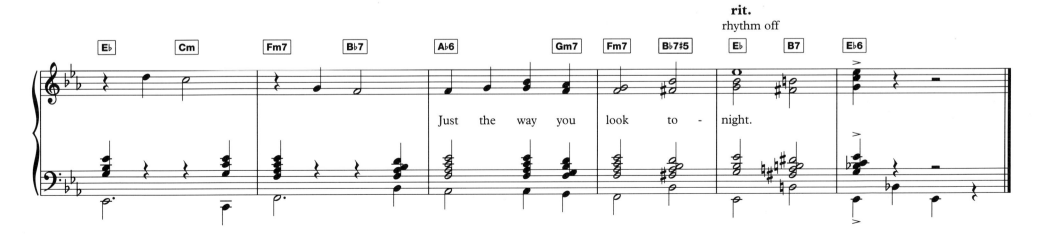

35

WHERE DO I BEGIN?
(Love Story)

Words by CARL SIGMAN
Music by FRANCIS ALBERT LAI

Registration
Upper: Pop Organ or Orch. Strings
Lower: Piano / Organ / Strings
Pedal: Electric Bass
Rhythm   8 Beat
Tempo   ♩ = 80

38

WITH YOU I'M BORN AGAIN

Words by CAROL CONNERS
Music by DAVID SHIRE

Registration
Upper: Piano / Strings
Lower: Organ / Strings
Pedal: 8' Acoustic Bass
Rhythm Jazz Waltz or Waltz
Tempo ♩ = 90

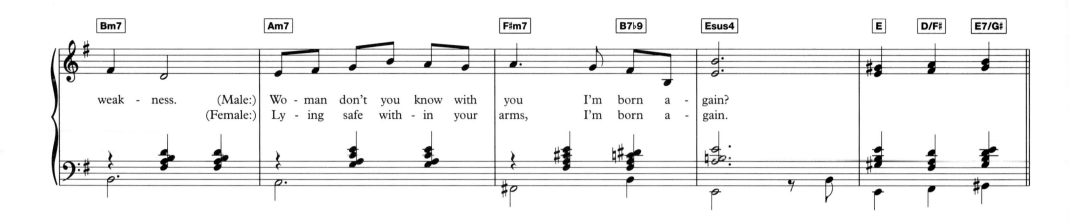

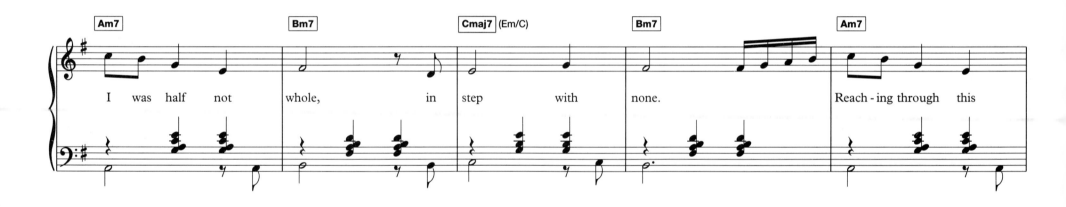

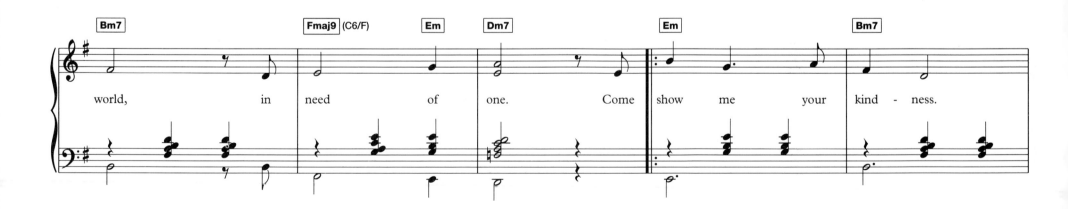

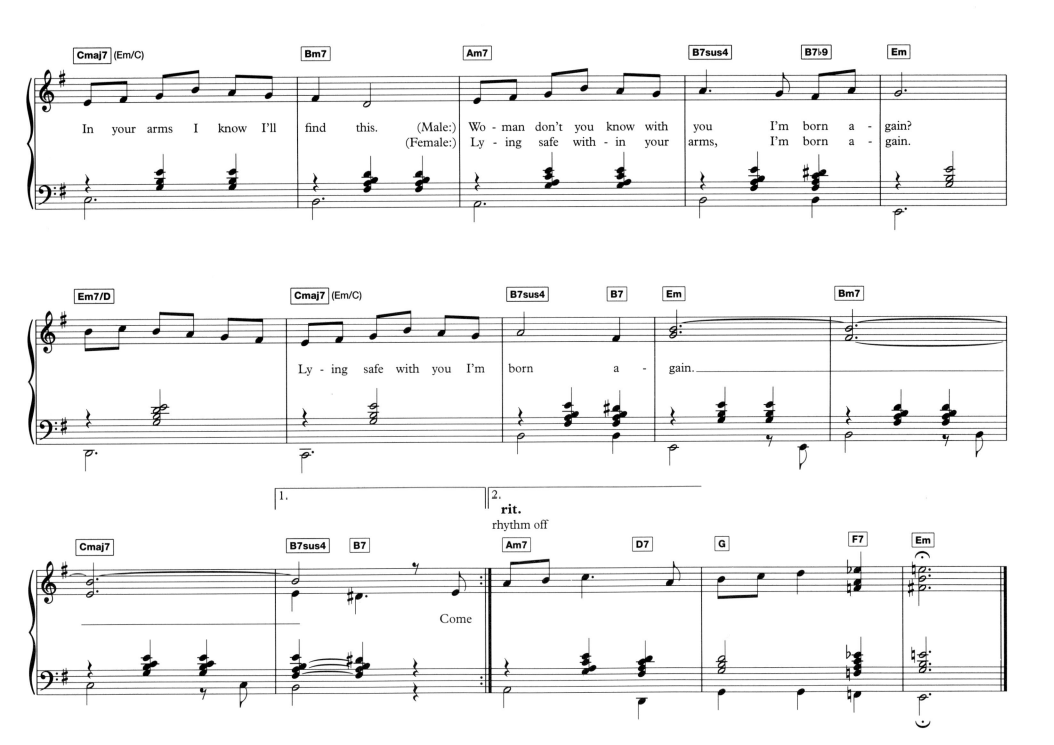

YOU LIGHT UP MY LIFE

Words and Music by JOE BROOKS

Registration
Upper: Oboe / Strings
Lower: Electric Piano / Strings
Pedal: 8' Acoustic Bass
Rhythm   Waltz
Tempo   ♩ = 84

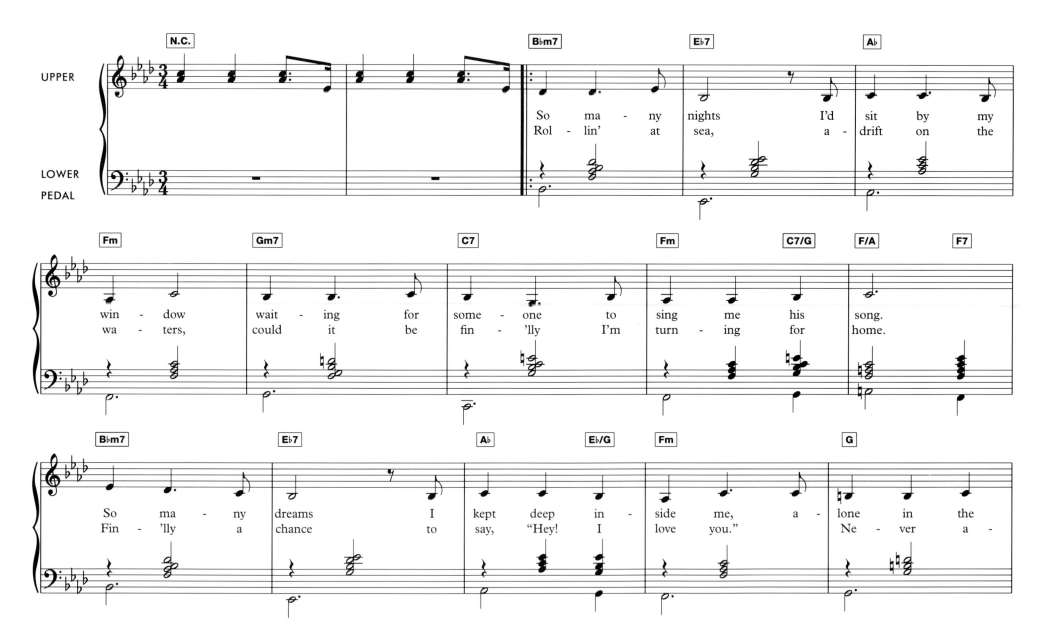

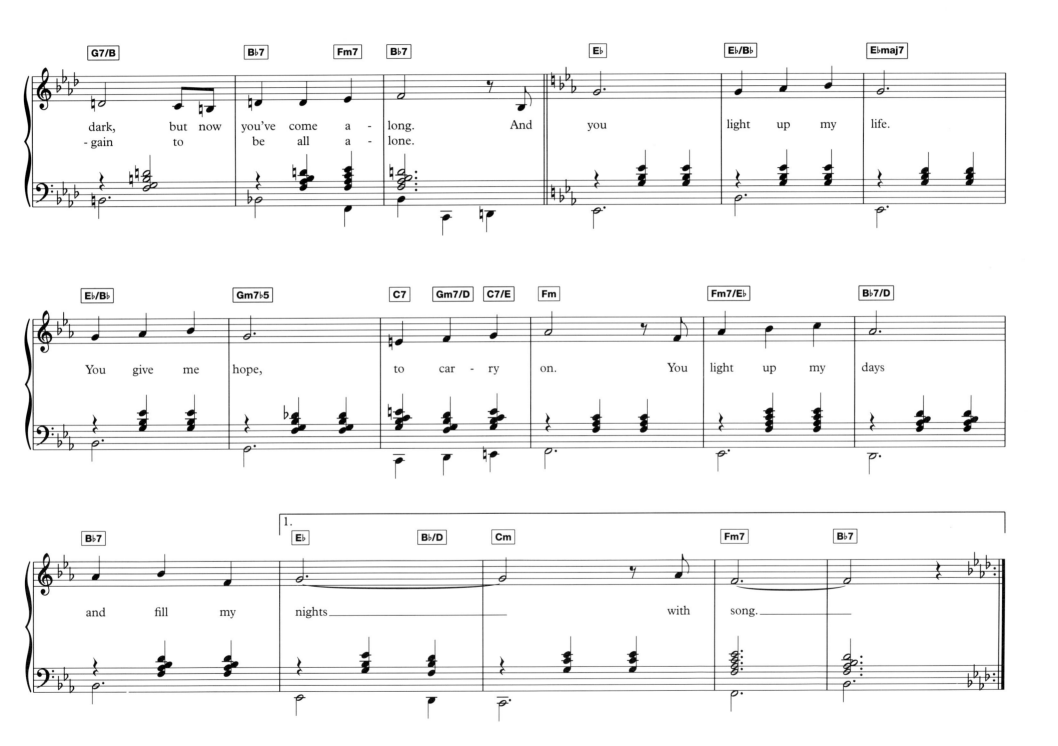

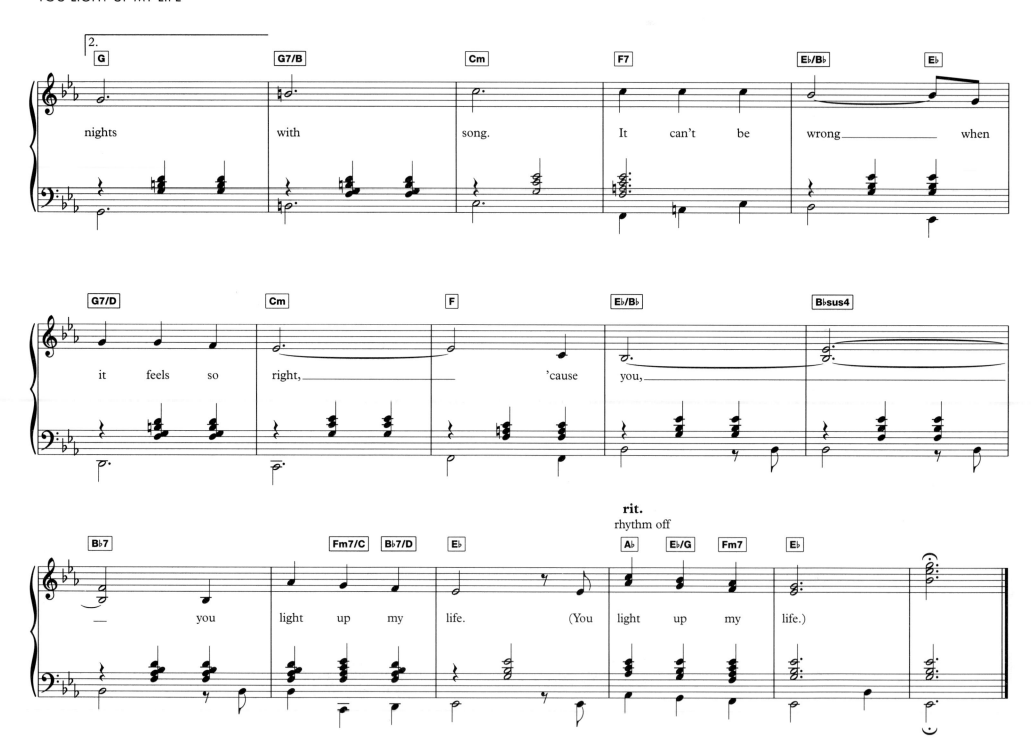

YOU'LL NEVER KNOW

Words by MACK GORDON
Music by HARRY WARREN

Registration
Upper: Pop Organ or Brass
Lower: Organ / Strings
Pedal: 8' Acoustic Bass
Rhythm: Bounce or Swing, (Final Chorus) Slow Rock
Tempo: ♩ = 90

Printed in England
Panda Press · Haverhill · Suffolk · 2/96

also available in this series:

All Time Standards

Bewitched   Moon River
Cheek To Cheek   The Nearness Of You
Crazy Rhythm   Secret Love
I Remember You   September Song
It's Magic   Someone To Watch Over Me
It's Only A Paper Moon   That Old Black Magic
Mona Lisa   When I Fall In Love
You Make Me Feel So Young

Order Ref: 3509A

Showtunes

Almost Like Being In Love   Getting To Know You
Anything Goes   Hello Dolly!
Bali Ha'i   I've Grown Accustomed To Her Face
Cabaret   My Favorite Things
The Colors Of My Life   Oh, What A Beautiful Mornin'
Consider Yourself   Smoke Gets In Your Eyes
A Foggy Day   They Can't Take That Away From Me
You'll Never Walk Alone

Order Ref: 3512A

Film Hits

Alfie   I Have Nothing
Arthur's Theme (Best That You Can Do)   (I've Had) The Time Of My Life
Big Spender   La Bamba
Bright Eyes   Raindrops Keep Fallin' On My Head
Endless Love   The Sound Of Music
Evergreen   Star Wars (Main Theme)
For Your Eyes Only   Summer Holiday
Tara's Theme

Order Ref: 3510A

Easy Listening

Always On My Mind   Laughter In The Rain
Chanson D'Amour   Moonlighting
Earth Angel   Now And Forever
Everybody's Talkin'   The Rose
Goodbye Girl   Trains And Boats And Planes
If I Were A Carpenter   We Don't Cry Out Loud
It's All In The Game   Why Do Fools Fall In Love?
You Make Me Feel Brand New

Order Ref: 3513A

Love Songs

I Can't Give You Anything But Love   Tenderly
I Just Called To Say I Love You   Three Times A Lady
I'll Be There   Too Marvellous For Words
Killing Me Softly With His Song   Up Where We Belong
Let's Do It (Let's Fall In Love)   The Way You Look Tonight
Love Is A Many-Splendoured Thing   Where Do I Begin? (Love Story)
Love Is Here To Stay   With You I'm Born Again
My Foolish Heart   You Light Up My Life
You'll Never Know

Order Ref: 3511A

Solid Gold Hits

Don't Let The Sun Go Down On Me   Oh, Pretty Woman
Eternal Flame   The Power Of Love
A Horse With No Name   Save The Best For Last
Hotel California   Solitaire
I Got You Babe   Stand By Me
Nights In White Satin   What A Wonderful World
A Whiter Shade Of Pale

Order Ref: 3514A